Salvation By Faith

John Wesley's Sermon

In Today

Copyright 2012 1

First Edition Published in   ublishing

Contents

Translator's preface

John Wesley led one of the greatest Christian revivals in the history of England, and his open air preaching saw many thousands of conversions all across Great Britain. The 'Forty-Four Sermons' which he compiled for use by Methodist Local Preachers remains a timeless classic, and a definitive collection of core Wesleyan doctrine, along with his Notes on the New Testament.

Forty-Four Sermons was first published in 1759, over 250 years ago, and since then the English language has changed and evolved to the point that his works can no longer be easily read and understood in their original dialect. Therefore to preserve Wesley's message and to allow it to come to life for a new generation, this project has been undertaken.

Many of John and Charles Wesley's views can be seen as products of the day and age in which they lived. The passion they preached with, and the relentless conviction behind their words changed Britain, some say prevented a civil uprising and revolution, and in many ways influenced the whole world. However, by today's standards, certain parts of their preaching might in places come across as uncomfortable, questionable, or even downright offensive to some readers, the modern church being as broad and diverse in theological variety as it is.

I would firstly like to state that anything I have translated and paraphrased into the modern vernacular from Wesley's writings does not necessarily represent my views, but rather the views of the original writer, in the setting of their culture and place in history. I would secondly like to state that I have not reproduced these writings with any agenda, but rather for the sake of devotional study and academic curiosity concerning their doctrines and beliefs.

The sermons are translated sentence by sentence, carefully and prayerfully. The aim has been to communicate both word-for-word and thought-for-thought, choosing clarity of communication in simple English over archaic sentence structure where necessary, and preferring the original word order when there is no difference.

Wesley used the King James Bible in his original sermons, whereas to remain consistent with the word-for-word and thought-for-thought method used in these translations, the New International Version and New Living Translation have been used instead. Gender inclusive language has also been favoured over the archaic use of the word 'he' to indicate 'everyone'. The word 'humanity' has also been favoured over the word 'mankind', as this latter word now carries with it gender implications which were not present in Wesley's time. The complete original sermon is also included. Each time scripture is directly quoted, it is italicised.

Each sermon will be translated and published in order, from 1 to 44, and when the series is completed, they will be published as one volume.

In the meantime, I hope you are blessed, encouraged and challenged by the message of John Wesley, the man who completely changed the nation in which he lived. I hope you are spurred on to a zealous faith as you read how radical he was, and look back on the incredible fruit which his approach to Christian living bore for the Kingdom of God.

In Christ,

James Hargreaves

Salvation By Faith (In Today's English)

Sermon 1 of 44

Introduction

Preached at St Mary's, Oxford, before the University, on June 11th, 1738.[1]

'It is by grace you have been saved, through faith – and this is not from yourselves, it is the gift of God – not by works, so that no-one can boast.' (Eph 2:8-9)

1:1. All the blessings which God has given to humanity come simply from his grace, generosity or favour; His free, undeserved favour. His favour is undeserved in every way, because no-one can claim that God owes them even the least of His mercies. It was freely given grace that *'formed a man*

---

[1]   Wesley recorded the date as June 18; but he was then in Holland. See Journal. It was delivered on June 11.

from the dust of the ground and breathed into his nostrils the breath of life' (Gen 2:7), and stamped on that soul the image of God, and put all things under his feet.[2]

That same freely given grace is also given to us this very day as we live and breathe, and it is given to all things. For there is nothing which we can be, have or do which can entitle us to the least gift from God.

Isaiah 26:12 states: *'Lord... all that we have accomplished you have done for us'*. All humanity's accomplishments, therefore, are yet more instances of God's free mercy: and whatever righteousness may be found in people, this is also the gift of God.[3]

---

[2]   1. All the blessings which God hath bestowed upon man are of his mere grace, bounty, or favour; his free, undeserved favour; favour altogether undeserved; man having no claim to the least of his mercies. It was free grace that "formed man of the dust of the ground, and breathed into him a living soul," and stamped on that soul the image of God, and "put all things under his feet."

[3]   The same free grace continues to us, at this day, life, and breath, and all things. For there is nothing we are, or have, or do, which can deserve the least thing at God's hand. "All our works, Thou, O God,

1:2. If this is the case, how then can a sinful person be forgiven by God for even the least of his sins? Can any good work be enough? No. No matter how many good works someone does, no matter how holy those works are, they don't originate with the person, but with God. Indeed, all of us are unholy and sinful in our natural selves, and all of us need something new to reconcile us to God.[4]

Jesus said *'every good tree bears good fruit, but a bad tree bears bad fruit'* (Mt 7:17). We cannot bear good fruit on our own, we are all therefore bad trees. The human heart is altogether corrupt and loathsome, we *'all have sinned and fall short of the glory of God'* (Rom 3:23), - that glorious natural goodness initially placed in the human soul, in the image of the great Creator. Therefore, because we have

---

hast wrought in us." These, therefore, are so many more instances of free mercy: and whatever righteousness may be found in man, this is also the gift of God.

[4]   2. Wherewithal then shall a sinful man atone for any the least of his sins With his own works No. Were they ever so many or holy, they are not his own, but God's. But indeed they are all unholy and sinful themselves, so that every one of them needs a fresh atonement.

nothing at all to offer: no inherent righteousness nor good works, we can neither claim nor demand any good thing from God.[5]

1:3. If we sinful people nevertheless receive good things from God; we are receiving undeserved blessings, multiplied many times over! If God still graciously pours his daily blessings upon us, along with the very greatest blessing of all, the saving of our souls, how can we say anything but 'Thank God for His inexpressible gift!'[6]

And this is the way it truly is. This is how God shows us the quality of his love for us; though we were unholy and

---

[5]   Only corrupt fruit grows on a corrupt tree. And his heart is altogether corrupt and abominable; being "come short of the glory of God," the glorious righteousness at first impressed on his soul, after the image of his great Creator. Therefore, having nothing, neither righteousness nor works, to plead, his mouth is utterly stopped before God.

[6]   3. If then sinful men find favour with God, it is "grace upon grace!" If God vouchsafe still to pour fresh blessings upon us, yea, the greatest of all blessings, salvation; what can we say to these things, but, "Thanks be unto God for his unspeakable gift!"

unrighteous, Christ died to save us. It is the freely given, undeserved gift of God that we can be saved by believing in him. Being saved does depend on us having faith in God, but we can only be saved because God gives us that faith as a free gift.[7]

1:4. Now, so that we do not fall from the grace of God, we must carefully ask, -

1. What Kind Of Faith Do We Need To Be Saved?

2. What Is Faith Saving Us From?

and

3. How May We May Some Common Objections?[8]

---

[7]   And thus it is. herein "God commendeth his love toward us, in that, while we were yet sinners, Christ died" to save us "By grace" then "are ye saved through faith." Grace is the source, faith the condition, of salvation.

[8]   Now, that we fall not short of the grace of God, it concerns us carefully to inquire, --
  I. What faith it is through which we are saved.
  II. What is the salvation which is through faith.
  III. How we may answer some objections.

What Kind Of Faith Do We Need To Be Saved?

2:1. Firstly, saving faith is not merely simplistic 'Heathen Faith'. God requires those who have not heard of him (Heathens), to accept that He exists, and to believe that he will reward those who diligently seek Him. He requires them to seek him by recognising and worshiping Him as God, giving Him thanks for all things, and by carefully practicing right behaviour, justice, mercy and honesty towards one another. In Jesus' time, a Greek, Roman, Scythian or Indian who had never heard of the true God was nevertheless without excuse before Him if they did not at least believe these basics; the existence of God, His basic characteristics, future reward and punishment, and their obligation to live in a morally upright way. This is the definition of basic 'Heathen Faith'.[9]

---

[9]   1. And, first, it is not barely the faith of a heathen. Now, God requireth of a heathen to believe, "that God is; that he is a rewarder of them that diligently seek him;" and that he is to be sought by glorifying him as God, by giving him thanks for all things, and by a careful practice

2:2. Nor, secondly, is the faith we need a 'Demon's Faith' (although a demon's faith goes much further than Heathen Faith), for the demons not only believe that there is a wise and powerful God who rewards generously and punishes justly, but also that Jesus is the Son of God, the Christ, the Saviour of the world. In Luke 4:34 the demon explicitly says to Jesus, '*I know who you are-the Holy One of God!*'[10]

There is no doubt that the unhappy demon believed every word which came out of the mouth of the Holy One, and all that was written by the holy men in the past. In Acts 16:17, a demon was compelled to tell the glorious truth about two of those holy men, Paul and Silas, saying *'These men are*

---

of moral virtue, of justice, mercy, and truth, toward their fellow creatures. A Greek or Roman, therefore, yea, a Scythian or Indian, was without excuse if he did not believe thus much: the being and attributes of God, a future state of reward and punishment, and the obligatory nature of moral virtue. For this is barely the faith of a heathen.

[10]   2. Nor, secondly, is it the faith of a devil, though this goes much farther than that of a heathen. For the devil believes, not only that there is a wise and powerful God, gracious to reward, and just to punish; but also, that Jesus is the Son of God, the Christ, the Saviour of the world. So we find him declaring, in express terms, "I know Thee who Thou art; the Holy One of God" (Luke 4:34).

servants of the Most High God, who are telling you the way to be saved!'[11]

These things then are believed even by the great enemy of both God and humanity, who trembles at what he believes; that God lived on earth as a man, that He will crush all his enemies under His feet, and that all Scripture is inspired by God. This is the extent of a 'Demon's Faith'.[12]

2:3. Thirdly, 'Saving Faith' (which will be explained next) is not even the faith which the Apostles themselves had while Christ was still upon the earth; even though they believed in Him enough to leave everything and follow Him, even though they had power to perform miracles, to heal every

---

[11]   Nor can we doubt but that unhappy spirit believes all those words which came out of the mouth of the Holy One, yea, and whatsoever else was written by those holy men of old, of two of whom he was compelled to give that glorious testimony, "These men are the servants of the most high God, who show unto you the way of salvation."
[12]   Thus much, then, the great enemy of God and man believes, and trembles in believing, --that God was made manifest in the flesh; that he will "tread all enemies under his feet;" and that "all Scripture was given by inspiration of God." Thus far goeth the faith of a devil.

kind of sickness and any type of disease. They even had

power and authority over all demons, and greatest of all,

were sent by Jesus, their Master to peach the Kingdom of

God.[13]

2.4. What kind of faith do we need then to be saved? First

and foremost, in its most basic form it is faith in Christ.

Christ and the God He described to us are those whom

saving faith must be placed in. This is how saving faith is

thoroughly and completely different to 'Heathen Faith',

ancient or modern. It is also entirely different to a 'Demon's

Faith', because it is not merely a formal, logical thing; a

cold, lifeless acceptance of data, a set of equations in one's

head, but also a matter of ones' heart. This can be seen in the

---

[13]   3. Thirdly. The faith through which we are saved, in that sense of the word which will hereafter be explained, is not barely that which the Apostles themselves had while Christ was yet upon earth; though they so believed on him as to "leave all and follow him;" although they had then power to work miracles, to "heal all manner of sickness, and all manner of disease;" yea, they had then "power and authority over all devils;" and, which is beyond all this, were sent by their Master to "preach the kingdom of God."

Scriptures, where it is written: *'If you declare with your mouth, "Jesus is Lord", and believe in your heart that God raised him from the dead, you will be saved'* (Rom 10:9).[14]

2:5. And it is different faith to that which the Apostles themselves held while our Lord was on earth, in that it must acknowledge that his death was essential, that it was the only thing good enough to save us, and it must acknowledge the power of His resurrection. It must accept that Jesus' death is the only offering great enough to redeem humanity from eternal destruction, and that His resurrection is the only thing great enough to restore life and immortality to us all. As Paul

---

[14]   4. What faith is it then through which we are saved It may be answered, first, in general, it is a faith in Christ: Christ, and God through Christ, are the proper objects of it. herein, therefore, it is sufficiently, absolutely distinguished from the faith either of ancient or modern heathens. And from the faith of a devil it is fully distinguished by this: it is not barely a speculative, rational thing, a cold, lifeless assent, a train of ideas in the head; but also a disposition of the heart. For thus saith the Scripture, "With the heart man believeth unto righteousness;" and, "If thou shalt confess with thy mouth the Lord Jesus, and shalt believe in thy heart that God hath raised him from the dead, thou shalt be saved."

wrote; *'He was delivered over to death for our sins and was raised to life for our justification'* (Rom 4:25).[15]

Christian faith then, not only must accept the entire Biblical truth about Christ, but also acknowledge its complete dependence on the blood of Christ to be saved. It must trust that his life, death and resurrection were enough to save. It must rest and rely completely upon Him as our means of reconciliation to God, and as our reason to live. He was given for us, He lives in us, and because we have died with him, and bound ourselves to him, His wisdom, righteousness, holiness and ransom become ours. These four things can be summed up in one word: salvation (which means, being saved).[16]

---

[15]   5. And herein does it differ from that faith which the Apostles themselves had while our Lord was on earth, that it acknowledges the necessity and merit of his death, and the power of his resurrection. It acknowledges his death as the only sufficient means of redeeming man from death eternal, and his resurrection as the restoration of us all to life and immortality; inasmuch as he "was delivered for our sins, and rose again for our justification."

[16]   Christian faith is then, not only an assent to the whole gospel of Christ, but also a full reliance on the blood of Christ; a trust in the merits

of his life, death, and resurrection; a recumbency upon him as our atonement and our life, as given for us, and living in us; and, in consequence hereof, a closing with him, and cleaving to him, as our "wisdom, righteousness, sanctification, and redemption," or, in one word, our salvation.

What This Salvation Actually Is

3:1. First of all, whatever else it may be, it is for this present day. It is something attainable, yes - it can actually be received here on earth by those who have this faith. Paul the Apostle said to the believers in Ephesus, and to all Christians for all time, not 'you will one day be saved by your faith' (although that is also true), but 'you ARE saved through faith'.[17]

3:2. You are saved (to boil everything down into just one word) from sin. This is what we are saved from by saving, Christian faith. This is the great salvation which was predicted by the Angel of the Lord, before God brought His unique Son into the world: *'You are to give him the name*

---

[17]   1. And, First, whatsoever else it imply, it is a present salvation. It is something attainable, yea, actually attained, on earth, by those who are partakers of this faith. For thus saith the Apostle to the believers at Ephesus, and in them to the believers of all ages, not, Ye shall be (though that also is true), but, "Ye are saved through faith."

Jesus, because he will save his people from their sins' (Mt 1:21).[18]

And neither here, nor anywhere else in the Holy Scriptures is there any limitation or restriction on this. *'He will save his people'*, or, as it states elsewhere, *'all who believe in Him'* will be saved from all their sins, including their naturally sinful state, and their actual sinful acts, including all sins of the past and the present, and every sin of the body and the spirit. By true faith in Jesus, they are saved from both the actual guilt of sin and from the power that guilt has over them.[19]

---

[18]   2. Ye are saved (to comprise all in one word) from sin. This is the salvation which is through faith. This is that great salvation foretold by the angel, before God brought his First-begotten into the world: "Thou shalt call his name Jesus; for he shall save his people from their sins."

[19]   And neither here, nor in other parts of holy writ, is there any limitation or restriction. All his people, or, as it is elsewhere expressed, "all that believe in him," he will save from all their sins; from original and actual, past and present sin, "of the flesh and of the spirit." Through faith that is in him, they are saved both from the guilt and from the power of it.

3:3. They are saved first from the actual guilt of all past sin. All the world stands guilty before God, so much so that the Psalmist writes *'Lord, if you kept a record of our sins, who, O Lord, could ever survive?'* (Ps 130:3).

As Paul points out, even the Old Testament makes us aware of our guilt, but offers nothing to rescue us from it: *'no-one will be declared righteous in his sight by observing the law'* (Rom 3:20).

But now, *'righteousness from God comes through faith in Jesus Christ to all who believe'* (Rom 3:21).

Now, God's people are made righteous in His sight, freely and without deserving it, through the great ransom paid by Jesus Christ: *'God presented Jesus as the sacrifice for sin. People are made right with God when they believe that Jesus sacrificed his life, shedding his blood. This sacrifice shows that God was being fair when he held back and did not*

punish those who sinned in times past' (Rom 3:25).

'Christ redeemed us from the curse of the law by becoming a

curse for us' (Gal 3:13).

He *'cancelled the written code, with its regulations, that was*

against us and that stood opposed to us; he took it away,

nailing it to the cross' (Col 2:14).

'Therefore there is now no condemnation for those who are

in Christ Jesus' (Rom 8:1).[20]

---

[20]   3. First. From the guilt of all past sin: for, whereas all the world is guilty before God, insomuch that should he "be extreme to mark what is done amiss, there is none that could abide it;" and whereas, "by the law is" only "the knowledge of sin," but no deliverance from it, so that, "by" fulfilling "the deeds of the law, no flesh can be justified in his sight": now, "the righteousness of God, which is by faith of Jesus Christ, is manifested unto all that believe." Now, "they are justified freely by his grace, through the redemption that is in Jesus Christ." "Him God hath set forth to be a propitiation through faith in his blood, to declare his righteousness for (or by) the remission of the sins that are past." Now hath Christ taken away "the curse of the law, being made a curse for us." he hath "blotted out the handwriting that was against us, taking it out of the way, nailing it to his cross." "There is therefore no condemnation now to them which" believe "in Christ Jesus."

3:4. Now that Christ's people are saved from guilt, they are next saved from fear. Not from the fear a child has of offending their father, but from the kind of fear a slave has: a tormenting fear of punishment – fear of the wrath of God. They no longer regard him as a severe Master, but as a generous Father. *'You have not received a spirit that makes you fearful slaves. Instead, you received God's Spirit when he adopted you as his own children. Now we call him, "Abba, Father" For his Spirit joins with our spirit to affirm that we are God's children'* (Rom 8:15-16)[21]

They are also saved from the fear (though not from the possibility) of falling away from the grace of God, and thereby missing out on His great and precious promises.

---

[21]   4. And being saved from guilt, they are saved from fear. Not indeed from a filial fear of offending; but from all servile fear; from that fear which hath torment; from fear of punishment; from fear of the wrath of God, whom they now no longer regard as a severe Master, but as an indulgent Father. "They have not received again the spirit of bondage, but the Spirit of adoption, whereby they cry, Abba, Father: the Spirit itself also bearing witness with their spirits, that they are the children of God."

Thus they have peace with God through our Lord Jesus Christ (Rom 5:1), they boast in the hope of the glory of God (Rom 5:2b), and the love of God is poured out into their hearts, through the Holy Spirit, who has been given to them (Rom 5:5). Because of this, they are convinced (although perhaps not always as permanently or deeply) that *'neither death nor life, neither angels nor demons, neither the present nor the future, nor any powers, neither height nor depth, nor anything else in all creation, will be able to separate [them] from the love of God that is in Christ Jesus our Lord'* (Rom 8:38-39).[22]

---

[22] They are also saved from the fear, though not from the possibility, of falling away from the grace of God, and coming short of the great and precious promises. Thus have they "peace with God through our Lord Jesus Christ. They rejoice in hope of the glory of God. And the love of God is shed abroad in their hearts, through the Holy Ghost, which is given unto them." And hereby they are persuaded (though perhaps not at all times, nor with the same fullness of persuasion), that "neither death, nor life, nor things present, nor things to come, nor height, nor depth, nor any other creature, shall be able to separate them from the love of God, which is in Christ Jesus our Lord."

3:5. Through this saving faith they are not only saved from the power of guilt, but also from the power of the actual sin itself. It is just as John the Apostle writes: *'He appeared that he might take away our sins. And in him there is no sin. No-one who lives in him keeps on sinning'* (1 John 3:5-6), and also: *'Dear children, do not let anyone lead you astray... he who does what is sinful is of the devil'* (1 John 3:7a, 8a).[23]

Whoever believes is born of God, and *'no-one who is born of God will continue to sin, because God's seed remains in him; he cannot go on sinning, because he has been born of God'* (1 John 3:9), and once again: *'We know that anyone born of God does not continue to sin; the one who was born of God keeps him safe, and the evil one cannot harm him'* (1 John 5:18).[24]

---

[23]   5. Again: through this faith they are saved from the power of sin, as well as from the guilt of it. So the Apostle declares, "Ye know that he was manifested to take away our sins; and in him is no sin. Whosoever abideth in him sinneth not" (1 John 3:5ff.). Again, "Little children, let no man deceive you. he that committeth sin is of the devil.
[24]   Whosoever believeth is born of God. And whosoever is born of God doth not commit sin; for his seed remaineth in him: and he cannot

3:6. Someone who is born of God by faith, does not sin in the following ways:

Firstly, they do not commit habitual sin, because if it is a habit that they cannot break, it is ruling that person, and sin cannot rule in the heart of any believer.

Secondly they do not commit any intentional sin, because their will (while they remain Christian) is completely opposed to any and every sin, and finds it as horrifying as deadly poison.

Thirdly they do not desire any sinful thing, because they continually want the holy and perfect will of God, and any time they lean towards an unholy desire, by the grace of God they strangle that desire as soon as it begins.

---

sin, because he is born of God." Once more: "We know that whosoever is born of God sinneth not; but he that is begotten of God keepeth himself, and that wicked one toucheth him not" (1 John 5:18).

Fourthly, no-one who is too ill to control their actions, words or thoughts can sin, because they have no voluntary choice in their behaviour, and without this they cannot truly sin. Therefore we can see that anyone born of God does not sin, and while they cannot say that they have never sinned, now they sin no longer.[25]

3:7. This, then is the salvation which comes through faith, even now in the world today. It means being saved from sin and from the consequences of sin, both of which are often expressed in the word 'justification'. This word, taken in its broadest sense, implies release from guilt and punishment as the power of Jesus' death and resurrection is applied to the

---

[25] 6. he that is, by faith, born of God sinneth not (1.) by any habitual sin; for all habitual sin is sin reigning: But sin cannot reign in any that believeth. Nor (2.) by any wilful sin: for his will, while he abideth in the faith, is utterly set against all sin, and abhorreth it as deadly poison. Nor (3.) By any sinful desire; for he continually desireth the holy and perfect will of God. and any tendency to an unholy desire, he by the grace of God, stifleth in the birth. Nor (4.) Doth he sin by infirmities, whether in act, word, or thought; for his infirmities have no concurrence of his will; and without this they are not properly sins. Thus, "he that is born of God doth not commit sin": and though he cannot say he hath not sinned, yet now "he sinneth not."

soul of the sinner who now believes in Him. As Christ dwells in the believer's heart, they are delivered from the power of sin. Therefore, anyone who is justified in this way, i.e. saved by faith, has indeed been born again. They have been reborn through the Holy Spirit, and have begun a new life, which is *'hidden with Christ in God'* (Col 3:3).[26]

As newborn babies of the faith, they gladly receive the *'pure spiritual milk'* of the word (1 Pet 2:2), and through it they grow, becoming stronger in through the Lord their God, from faith to greater faith, from grace to greater grace, until after a long time, they become perfect people, *'measuring up to the full and complete standard of Christ'* (Eph 4:13).[27]

---

[26] 7. This then is the salvation which is through faith, even in the present world: a salvation from sin, and the consequences of sin, both often expressed in the word justification; which, taken in the largest sense, implies a deliverance from guilt and punishment, by the atonement of Christ actually applied to the soul of the sinner now believing on him, and a deliverance from the power of sin, through Christ formed in his heart. So that he who is thus justified, or saved by faith, is indeed born again. he is born again of the Spirit unto a new life, which "is hid with Christ in God."

[27] And as a new-born babe he gladly receives the adolon, "sincere milk of the word, and grows thereby;" going on in the might of the Lord

his God, from faith to faith, from grace to grace, until at length, he come unto "a perfect man, unto the measure of the stature of the fullness of Christ."

Responses To The Usual Objections

4:1. A common objection is that to preach salvation or justification by faith alone is to suggest there is no need for holiness and good works. To this objection I give this short answer: 'that would be true if we preached, as some do, a faith which is completely independent of those things, but we do not. We preach a faith which **produces** every good work, and all holiness.'[28]

4:2. It may be worthwhile to expand upon this, especially because it is not a new objection, but one as old as Paul the Apostle's time. Even then it was asked, *'If we emphasize faith, does this mean we can forget about the law?'* (Rom 3:31)[29]

---

[28] 1. The first usual objection to this is, that to preach salvation or justification, by faith only, is to preach against holiness and good works. To which a short answer might be given: "It would be so, if we spake, as some do, of a faith which was separate from these; but we speak of a faith which is not so, but productive of all good works, and all holiness."

[29] 2. But it may be of use to consider it more at large; especially since it is no new objection, but as old as St. Paul's time. For even then it

We answer firstly, that all of those who preach that obeying the law makes us right with God are clearly making that same law totally invalid. They do this openly and shamelessly, by adding extra rules and comments which remove the true meaning from the text, or they do it indirectly, by neglecting to point people to Christ, their only hope of ever being able to actually obey the whole law. We answer secondly, *'only when we have faith do we truly fulfil the law'* (Rom 3:31), both by showing its immense scope and depth of spiritual meaning, and by calling all to that way of life in which *'the just requirement of the law would be fully satisfied for us'* (Rom 8:4).[30]

---

was asked, "Do we not make void the law through faith"

[30]   We answer, First, all who preach not faith do manifestly make void the law; either directly and grossly, by limitations and comments that eat out all the spirit of the text; or indirectly, by not pointing out the only means whereby it is possible to perform it. Whereas, Secondly, "we establish the law," both by showing its full extent and spiritual meaning; and by calling all to that living way, whereby "the righteousness of the law may be fulfilled in them."

Those who have saving faith, while they trust only in Jesus' blood for their salvation, nevertheless study all the commands Christ gave, do all the good deeds which He has prepared in advance for them to do, and walk with Him so that they can enjoy having a good and Godly attitude, even having the same attitude which Jesus Himself had.[31]

4:3. The next objection we hear is this: Surely preaching that we do nothing and are yet accepted by God simply causes men to be proud? We answer, it might do so accidentally, so every believer should therefore take a serious warning from the words of the Apostle Paul, who said the natural branches in God's tree of faith (that is, unbelieving Jews) *were broken off because of unbelief, and you stand by faith. Do not be arrogant, but be afraid. For if God did not spare the*

---

[31] These, while they trust in the blood of Christ alone, use all the ordinances which he hath appointed, do all the "good works which he had before prepared that they should walk therein," and enjoy and manifest all holy and heavenly tempers, even the same mind that was in Christ Jesus.

natural branches, he will not spare you either' (Rom 11:21-22).[32]

Just look at how God is both very kind, and very severe! To those 'branches' who would not accept his Son, He was severe, but towards you who believe, He is kind for as long as you remain in His goodness (without which you too would be broken off). While you remain in the place where you can receive God's goodness, you should remember the words of the Apostle Paul, who knew this very objection was coming, and so provided an answer to it: *'Can we boast, then, that we have done anything to be accepted by God? No, because our acquittal is not based on obeying the law. It is based on faith'* (Rom 3:27).[33]

---

[32]   3. But does not preaching this faith lead men into pride We answer, Accidentally it may: therefore ought every believer to be earnestly cautioned, in the words of the great Apostle "Because of unbelief," the first branches "were broken off: and thou standest by faith. Be not high-minded, but fear. If God spared not the natural branches, take heed lest he spare not thee.

[33]   Behold therefore the goodness and severity of God! On them which fell, severity; but towards thee, goodness, if thou continue in his goodness; otherwise thou also shalt be cut off." And while he continues

If anyone could be made right with God by their perfect actions, then they would have the right to boast. No-one, however, who is *'counted as righteous, not because of their work, but because of their faith in God who forgives sinnners'* (Rom 4:5), has any right to boast.

Neither your faith nor your salvation actually come from yourselves, they are the gift of God; the free undeserved gift. He gives saving faith and salvation itself to us, because it makes Him happy to do so; He simply loves us. The ability to believe in Him is one undeserved gift from him, and the fact that believing saves us is yet another, *'not by works, so that no-one can boast'* (Eph 2:9).[34]

---

therein, he will remember those words of St. Paul, foreseeing and answering this very objection (Rom. 3:27), "Where is boasting then It is excluded. By what law of works Nay: but by the law of faith."

[34]   If a man were justified by his works, he would have whereof to glory. But there is no glorying for him "that worketh not, but believeth on him that justifieth the ungodly" (Rom. 4:5). To the same effect are the words both preceding and following the text (Eph. 2:4ff.): "God, who is rich in mercy, even when we were dead in sins, hath quickened us together with Christ (by grace ye are saved), that he might show the exceeding riches of his grace in his kindness toward us through Christ Jesus. For by grace are ye saved through faith; and that not of yourselves." Of yourselves cometh neither your faith nor your salvation:

This is because even our very best, most righteous works before believing in Christ, deserved nothing from God but condemnation. None of our works deserved God's gift of faith, and so therefore whoever has faith has done nothing to earn or deserve it. Nor are we saved because of the good works we do as believing Christians; because even those deeds are done by God through us, and when God rewards us for the good works which He Himself is actually doing through us, not only does He show how richly merciful He is, but He again leaves us no room whatsoever to boast.[35]

4:4. The next objection is this: Could talking this way about the free, un-earnable gifts of God, which save us or justify us

---

"it is the gift of God;" the free, undeserved gift; the faith through which ye are saved, as well as the salvation which he of his own good pleasure, his mere favour, annexes thereto. That ye believe, is one instance of his grace; that believing ye are saved, another. "Not of works, lest any man should boast."

[35]   For all our works, all our righteousness, which were before our believing, merited nothing of God but condemnation; so far were they from deserving faith, which therefore, whenever given, is not of works. Neither is salvation of the works we do when we believe, for it is then God that worketh in us: and, therefore, that he giveth us a reward for what he himself worketh, only commendeth the riches of his mercy, but leaveth us nothing whereof to glory.

freely by faith alone, actually encourage people to sin? Yes, it could and does: many will *'continue sinning so that God can show us more and more of his wonderful grace'* (Rom 6:1), but those people will be directly responsible for the wounds they are bringing on themselves.[36]

The goodness of God should lead believers to living in a Christ-like way, and it always will for any Christian who is sincere of heart. Sincere believers, when they know that they can be forgiven by Him, will cry out to Him to forgive and forget their sins too, through faith in Jesus. And if they are serious in their request, and do not give up, if they seek Him in all the ways He requires, and refuse to be satisfied until they find Him, *'He who is coming will come and will not delay'* (Heb 10:37).[37]

---

[36]   4. "However, may not the speaking thus of the mercy of God, as saving or justifying freely by faith only, encourage men in sin" Indeed, it may and will: Many will "continue in sin that grace may abound:" But their blood is upon their own head.

[37]   The goodness of God ought to lead them to repentance; and so it will those who are sincere of heart. When they know there is yet forgiveness with him, they will cry aloud that he would blot out their sins

He can do a great amount in a short time. The book of Acts is full of examples of God putting faith into people's hearts as quickly as lightning falls from the sky. Within an hour of Paul and Silas preaching to him, their jailer repented of his sins, believed in Christ, and was baptized. Three thousand people repented and believed on the day of Pentecost when the Apostle Peter preached. And, God be praised, there are many people today who are living proof that He is still 'mighty to save' in the same way as He was then.[38]

4:5. However, the same truth, looked at from another angle, raises a very different objection: 'If no-one can be saved, no matter what they do, then surely people will lose hope and

---

also, through faith which is in Jesus. And if they earnestly cry, and faint not, it they seek him in all the means he hath appointed; if they refuse to be comforted till he come; "he will come, and will not tarry."

[38]   And he can do much work in a short time. Many are the examples, in the Acts of the Apostles, of God's working this faith in men's hearts, even like lightning falling from heaven. So in the same hour that Paul and Silas began to preach, the jailer repented, believed, and was baptized; as were three thousand, by St. Peter, on the day of Pentecost, who all repented and believed at his first preaching And, blessed be God, there are now many living proofs that he is still "mighty to save."

begin to despair'. This is true, they might despair of being saved by their own works, by their own holiness, and so they should, because no-one can put their hope in the goodness of Christ until they have completely given up on hoping in their own goodness. Anyone who spends their time trying to be righteous on their own cannot receive the righteousness from God. That righteousness, which we receive through faith, cannot be given to anyone who hopes to become righteous by obeying rules.[39]

4:6. The final objection which some raise, is that salvation by faith alone is an uncomfortable belief. It is a shameless and utterly false lie from the devil to suggest such a thing. The truth is, it is actually the only comfortable belief. It is

---

[39]   5. Yet to the same truth, placed in another view, a quite contrary objection is made: "If a man cannot be saved by all that he can do, this will drive men to despair." True, to despair of being saved by their own works, their own merits, or righteousness. And so it ought; for none can trust in the merits of Christ, till he has utterly renounced his own. he that "goeth about to establish his own righteousness" cannot receive the righteousness of God. The righteousness which is of faith cannot be given him while he trusteth in that which is of the law.

profoundly comforting to all who recognise they have destroyed and condemned themselves by their own sins. Because *'anyone who trusts in him will never be disgraced'* (Rom 10:11), and our Lord who is over everyone *'gives generously to all who call on Him'* (Rom 10:12).[40]

Can this be? Mercy for everyone? For Zacchaeus, who publicly robbed his own people? For Mary Magdalene, a common prostitute? I think I hear someone say, 'then even I can hope for mercy!'

And you may indeed hope for it, you who are suffering and without comfort. God will not ignore your prayer. No, perhaps within the very hour He might say to you *'Be encouraged, my child! Your sins are forgiven'* (Mt 9:2), so

---

[40]   6. But this, it is said, is an uncomfortable doctrine. The devil spoke like himself, that is, without either truth or shame, when he dared to suggest to men that it is such. It is the only comfortable one, it is "very full of comfort," to all self-destroyed, self-condemned sinners. That "whosoever believeth on him shall not be ashamed that the same Lord over all is rich unto all that call upon him"

that being forgiven, your sins will rule you no longer. Then the Holy Spirit will join with your spirit to affirm that you are a child of God (Rom 8:16).[41]

What wonderful news! What joyful news, for everyone, everywhere! *'Come, all you who are thirsty, come to the waters, come, buy without money and without cost'* (Isa 55:1).

Whatever your sins are, though they are red like crimson, though they number more than the hairs on your head, come, return to the Lord and He will have mercy on you. Come to our God, because he will thoroughly pardon you.[42]

---

[41] here is comfort, high as heaven, stronger than death! What! Mercy for all For Zacchaeus, a public robber For Mary Magdalene, a common harlot Methinks I hear one say "Then I, even I, may hope for mercy!" And so thou mayest, thou afflicted one, whom none hath comforted! God will not cast out thy prayer. Nay, perhaps he may say the next hour, "Be of good cheer, thy sins are forgiven thee;" so forgiven, that they shall reign over thee no more; yea, and that "the Holy Spirit shall bear witness with thy spirit that thou art a child of God."

[42] O glad tidings! tidings of great joy, which are sent unto all people! "Ho, every one that thirsteth, come ye to the waters: Come ye, and buy, without money and without price." Whatsoever your sins be,

4:7. When there are no objections left, some people simply resort to saying that 'salvation by faith' is not a fundamentally important teaching, and should not be preached as the foundation message of the church. Some say it should not be taught at all, but what does the Holy Spirit have to say on the matter? *'No-one can lay any foundation other than the one we already have – Jesus Christ'* (1 Cor 3:11).

So if Jesus is the foundation, and if anyone who believes in Him will be saved, then surely these things must be the first thing we preach. Some might argue, 'that's all well and good, but this message isn't suitable for everyone'.[43]

"though red like crimson," though more than the hairs of your head, "return ye unto the Lord, and he will have mercy upon you, and to our God, for he will abundantly pardon."

[43]   7. When no more objections occur, then we are simply told that salvation by faith only ought not to be preached as the first doctrine, or, at least, not to be preached at all. But what saith the Holy Ghost "Other foundation can no man lay than that which is laid, even Jesus Christ." So then, that "whosoever believeth on him shall be saved," is, and must be, the foundation of all our preaching; that is, must be preached first. "Well, but not to all."

Well who then is the message of Christ unsuitable for? Who shall we exclude? Is it unsuitable for the poor? No, they have a special right to have the gospel preached to them. Is it unsuitable for the uneducated? No. God has given His message to uneducated and simple people from the beginning. What about young people then? In no way is it unsuitable for them, for Jesus said *'Let the children come to me. Don't stop them!'* (Mt 19:14)[44]

How about sinful people? They are the people who need to hear it the most! Jesus said *'I have not come to call the righteous, but sinners'* (Mk 2:17).

Well then, if we were to exclude anyone from our message, it would be those who are well educated, those with good

---

[44] To whom, then are we not to preach it Whom shall we except The poor Nay; they have a peculiar right to have the gospel preached unto them. The unlearned No. God hath revealed these things unto unlearned and ignorant men from the beginning. The young By no means. "Suffer these," in any wise, "to come unto Christ, and forbid them not."

reputations, those who have high moral standing. It is a fact that they too often actually exclude themselves from hearing God's message. Whether they do or not, we nevertheless must continue to preach the words of Jesus, because this is what our commission says: *'Go into all the world and preach the good news to everyone'* (Mk 16:15).

If anyone distorts that commission, or any part of it, they will bring ruin on themselves, which will be a burden that they must bear. But for us, as surely as God lives, whatever He commands us, we will say.[45]

---

45   The sinners Least of all. "He came not to call the righteous, but sinners to repentance." Why then, if any, we are to except the rich, the learned, the reputable, the moral men. And, it is true, they too often except themselves from hearing; yet we must speak the words of our Lord. For thus the tenor of our commission runs, "Go and preach the gospel to every creature." If any man wrest it, or any part of it, to his destruction, he must bear his own burden. But still, "as the Lord liveth, whatsoever the Lord saith unto us, that we will speak."

In Closing

5:1. Nowadays especially we will continue to preach that we are saved by grace through faith, because it has never been more important to maintain this teaching than it is today. Nothing but this can effectively stop the delusional Roman Catholic Church growing up among us. It would be an endless task to list all the errors of that church, one by one. Establishing that 'we are saved by faith alone' is what cuts out the root of that tree, and it falls down immediately when this is done. It was this teaching (which the Anglican church correctly calls the bedrock and foundation of the Christian faith) that first drove Pope Worship out of Britain, and this alone can keep it out.[46]

---

[46]   8. At this time, more especially, will we speak, that "by grace are ye saved through faith": because, never was the maintaining this doctrine more seasonable than it is at this day. Nothing but this can effectually prevent the increase of the Romish delusion among us. It is endless to attack, one by one, all the errors of that Church. But salvation by faith strikes at the root, and all fall at once where this is established. It was this doctrine, which our Church justly calls the strong rock and foundation of the Christian religion, that first drove Popery out of these kingdoms; and it is this alone can keep it out.

Nothing but this teaching can stop the tidal wave of immorality which has covered our country. Trying to discourage people from sinning through incentives or threats is as slow and ineffective as trying to empty the ocean one drop at a time, but the righteousness which comes from God by faith has the power to stop the ocean's proud waves. This is the only thing that can silence people who take pleasure in shameful behaviour, and openly deny the Lord who has paid the price for them. Some of these people can talk about their morals and rules as if they have been written by God Himself in their hearts. When one hears them speak in this way, it is easy to think that they might not be far from becoming truly Christian, but try to move on from discussing how society can be fixed by rules and laws, and begin discussing the gospel with them. Start by discussing how people are fixed only by the inner goodness that comes through faith in Christ, who is the end of the law to everyone who believes in Him, and those who seemed virtually, if not completely Christian expose themselves as bringers of ruin and damnation, as far from life and salvation as Hell is from Heaven. May God be merciful to them![47]

5:2. Whenever 'salvation by faith' is preached to the world, the Devil becomes enraged. He stirred up earth and hell to destroy those first early disciples, because they preached it. Knowing that 'salvation by faith alone' could turn his whole kingdom on it's head, he also summoned all his evil forces, and used every kind of lie and slander to frighten Martin Luther away from reviving it. We cannot be surprised by this, because as Luther, the man of God observed; 'How

---

[47]   Nothing but this can give a check to that immorality which hath "overspread the land as a flood." Can you empty the great deep, drop by drop Then you may reform us by dissuasives from particular vices. But let the "righteousness which is of God by faith be brought in, and so shall its proud waves be stayed. Nothing but this can stop the mouths of those who "glory in their shame, and openly deny the Lord that bought them." They can talk as sublimely of the law, as he that hath it written by God in his heart To hear them speak on this head might incline one to think they were not far from the kingdom of God: but take them out of the law into the gospel; begin with the righteousness of faith; with Christ, "the end of the law to every one that believeth;" and those who but now appeared almost, if not altogether, Christians, stand confessed the sons of perdition; as far from life and salvation (God be merciful unto them!) as the depth of hell from the height of heaven.

infuriating it must be for a proud, strong man, armed to the teeth, to be stopped in his tracks and made completely powerless by a little child with a twig in his hand!' especially when he knew that the child would certainly knock him down and trample on him.[48]

It is so, Lord Jesus! In this way Your strength has always been made perfect in weakness! Step out then, oh small child who believes in Christ, and you will *'go forth to perform awe-inspiring deeds!'* (Ps 45:4).

Although you are as helpless and weak as a newborn baby, the devil will fall down before you. You will overcome him,

---

[48]   9. For this reason the adversary so rages whenever "salvation by faith" is declared to the world: for this reason did he stir up earth and hell, to destroy those who first preached it. And for the same reason, knowing that faith alone could overturn the foundations of his kingdom, did he call forth all his forces, and employ all his arts of lies and calumny, to affright Martin Luther from reviving it. Nor can we wonder thereat; for, as that man of God observes, "How would it enrage a proud, strong man armed, to be stopped and set at nought by a little child coming against him with a reed in his hand!" especially when he knew that little child would surely overthrow him, and tread him under foot.

defeat him, throw him down, and trample on him. You will march onward, under the great Captain who has saved you, going from victory to victory, until all your enemies are destroyed and *'death is swallowed up in victory'* (1 Cor 15:54).[49]

Now, thank God that He has given us victory through our Lord Jesus Christ, to whom, along with the Father and the Holy Spirit, be blessing, glory, wisdom, thanks, honour, power and might for ever and ever. Amen.[50]

---

[49]   Even so, Lord Jesus! Thus hath Thy strength been ever "made perfect in weakness!" Go forth then, thou little child that believest in him, and his "right hand shall teach thee terrible things!" Though thou art helpless and weak as an infant of days, the strong man shall not be able to stand before thee. Thou shalt prevail over him, and subdue him, and overthrow him and trample him under thy feet. Thou shalt march on, under the great Captain of thy salvation, "conquering and to conquer," until all thine enemies are destroyed, and "death is swallowed up in victory."

[50]   Now, thanks be to God, which giveth us the victory through our Lord Jesus Christ; to whom, with the Father and the Holy Ghost, be blessing, and glory, and wisdom, and thanksgiving, and honour, and power, and might, for ever and ever. Amen

Printed in Great Britain
by Amazon

13142788R00037